By Cosmic Design

By Cosmic Design

Spirit Poems
(1974-2006)

by

John P. Cock

tranſcribe books

Dedicated
to
Universe Citizens
All

Contents

By Cosmic Design?

At Timberlake watching young people
gape as they hear Thomas say
the U.S. Constitution is destructive,
declaring only human rights;
or hearing him ask
now that western civilization
has passed through its religious
and humanist phases,
What next?

On the way forward from our past,
this cosmological age
highlights awesome seasons
that birth rituals
and daily sunrises and sunsets
that spiritize existence,
sanctifying early mornings
with meditation
and late evenings
with reverie:
    parents reading to and
    cuddling with their children,
    answering big questions,
    rubbing backs and humming
    as the little ones slip into
    earth's dark, sacred night

Are we not spiritual
    by cosmic design
and for cosmic reason?

Preface

I've been a poet ever since I memorized Psalms in Sunday school and the poem "Trees" in public school. My Granddaddy Cock used to quote poems when we'd visit him at his home or office.

Poetry's in the blood. But not only mine. We're all poets. We're crazy about songs, secular or religious. Think of all the poetic lyrics swirling in our beings, and at the strangest times popping up into consciousness and straight to tongue.

Later I got attached to the poems of D. H. Lawrence, Nikos Kazantzakis, e.e. cummings, Tagore, Lao Tzu, Rumi, and others. These poets tell a lot about me and what I like in poetry: substantial images about the transparent meaning of life, about what makes the world go round.

All language is poetry – even if it's prose – transmitting conscious reflection upon what's happening in creation. I like poems that have big contexts, deep insights that lean toward heart over mind – and sometimes poems written in lines that sing themselves.

When I read a Gerard Manley Hopkins' poem, I know my spirit has been juiced. When I read a Tagore poem I know I'm bound to the mystery. When I read Kazantzakis' *The Saviors of God*, my will collides with the will of my ancestors. When

I read Thomas Berry's writings I think in millennia terms. When I read a Jim Harrison poem I expect an image shower. And, for me, Mary Oliver's poems jump out of the heart of creation .

My poems are particularly about *spirit*, the most real thing there is (small "s" to mean we only commune with it in creation – not in some other world – and italicized to differentiate it from my spirit and all the other ways we use "spirit"), and how *it* occasions our great awakenments; our great preparation; our great work of care for the earth community; our great journey, that never-ending spirit journey we're all on.

Am I spooky religious? No. Am I "new age"? No. Am I liberal? No. Am I conservative? No. Do I dislike labels? Yes. I was raised in the western Christian tradition. It is my central stake, out from which I now swing in articulating the meaning of existence. But I'm not now traditionally religious, unless I say I'm from all the traditions of all my ancestors – therefore all traditions.

I'm just a human being who's aware of being on the great journey and wanting to share what I see and understand as the truth. Do I possess the truth? No. But I've received enough to live a rich and full life. Enough to share, I trust.

We can describe the century we've come out of as a time of getting clear on existence, life, creation – the way life is. The eye of the needle for us 20th-

21st century folk is *experience*. We have dared to see life as not some pre-created set of meanings to be believed and lived out, but of-the-moment experiences to be reflected upon deeply.

For me, then, good poetry comes out of one's swirl of experience, called his or her life in relationship with "10,000 things" (Taoism). What is my relationship to what's going on right here in front of me or way up in the atmosphere, and what do I name that mysterious power at the heart of all relationships in creation? Poetry, in large part for me, is about describing and naming that power as best I can, for it's the center of my experience and all reality.

You and I have had primal experiences that have revealed what life is all about. I have been convinced by these experiences that life is good, that life is on my side, that I'm especially glad to be here in my skin as who I am, that the total sweep of history has brought me to this point and therefore I'd rather have it as it is than not, and that ongoing, evolving creation gives me hope. This is the stuff of poetry for me, variations on these fundamental themes of truth. It's easy for me to say poetry is a profound medium.

A word about how this particular collection of poems is stitched together: for the most part, the poems come from my books in order of writing and publication (except the "9/11 Poems," which have not been printed in my books). Also, some of the poems are revised from their original publication. Some poems are new, born out of the prose of the book in that section.

Finally, these poems are compiled as a legacy for my children and grandchildren – and theirs, for a total of at least seven generations, I trust. I hope the poems will provide them a way to dialogue with the "old man," all their relationships in creation, and *spirit* at its heart.

July 2006   John P. Cock
                             Greensboro NC
                             USA

I

from *Called To Be:*
A Spirit Odyssey

Mama Dotte

She bore me
She nursed me
She cuddled me
She disciplined me
She exemplified strength
She listened to me
She supported me
She trusted me
She loved me

What I Learned In the Order:Ecumenical

To live simply
To love structure
To live on behalf of
To celebrate our living
To reflect on the mystery
To serve the shattered earth
To dream the impossible dream
To build the earth, the common earth

Joseph W. Mathews

called me
trained me
pushed me
priested me
assigned me
mystified me
motivated me
challenged me
emboldened me
communes in me

Marching Through the Night

Tune: *Les Bicyclettes de Belsize*

La, la, la . . .

O when Dark Night assaults my soul
    and nothing's presence fills the All,
And when the fire burns out my love, I suffer
    death before I die.

I am marching through the Night, silence and
    stillness, blackened light,
Trusting that Heaven will come at last and
    vanquish Hell.

Wounded so deep by awe I swoon, oppressive
    weakness seals my doom,
No place to hide, no will to live, I suffer death
    before I die.

I am marching through the Night,
    silence and stillness, searing light,
Mystery has won the war in me,
    I melt away.

I hear a voice, "You are my son;
    you are well-pleasing, blessed one!"
I am the one who's come to life,
    born of the fire before I die.

17

I am marching through the Night,
　　silence and stillness, filled with light,
Assured that Heaven has made
　　its shrine in darkest Hell.

And now Dark Night and I are friends;
　　I trust the Long March never ends,
For now I see by fire of love;
　　I've found the Way before I die.

I am marching through the Night,
　　silence and stillness, blazing light,
Leaping as one consumed by fire,
　　my passion born.

　　La, la, la . . . .

~Paris, 1974

This Understanding of Life

I am coming to understand that I do not have a
 soul, but exist in the soul of the creation;
that creation is blessed although we can destroy
 it, in part;
that science, in its materialistic deliberations,
 has left out the universal journey of con-
 sciousness and awareness of *spirit*,
 and the consequent I-we-it worldview
 has devalued our lives;
that *sin* is separation and parochialism;
that *salvation* is communion with what is;
that we humans are not the pinnacle of creation
 but share in the equality of all beings;
that the universe is always regenerating;
that revelation's been happening for billions of years
 and that the universal *Christ event*
 is at the heart of that revelatory process;
that grace motivates the universe,
 and faith in that grace is the
 authentic response of the creature;
that the communion of all beings is the universal
 sacred body, of which each institutional
 religious entity can be a microcosm –
 but is not automatically;
that love – the gift of grace – glues the universe
 together;
that the essence of love is sacrifice
 on behalf of any part of the universe.

Yet, I keep reminding myself
  – lest I devalue the way life *is* and relapse again
  into humanism thinking that I-we-it is all there is –
that everything has its context, even the universe.
And that the ultimate context will always be
  the *numinous*, eternal *spirit,*
  which alone has *no* referent.

This understanding of life seems quite enough.

Called To Be

I have rehearsed my life and found it good,
rich in experience,
planetary in orbit,
profound in depth,
wonder-full.

Do I wish I could live it over?
No, for what would I add?
Money, fame, things?
I have had love,
vocation,
collegiality,
adventure,
and
communion.

What is my secret?
No secret, but
from everlasting to everlasting
I Am called:
I am called to be.

~1997

II

from *The Transparent Event: Post-modern Christ Images*

The "No-Messiah Messiah"*

Stop waiting on another messiah.
Stop waiting for a miracle.
Stop waiting for anything.
The *Messiah* has already come.

This is *spirit's* mysterious and gracious trick:
if you're waiting on something to happen
before you start really living,
then "Guess what."

There is no messiah coming to save you,
and that fact is the *Messiah*.

It has already come.
It is here.
Lest you die waiting,
pick up your life and walk.
Now.

* Phrase from J. W. Mathews' *Christ of History*

I Wait for No Other

We are left with a big decision:
to live our given situation to the hilt
or to wait for some other.

Blasphemy is waiting on some other god to save us,
not believing that our one, true *God* already has.
Blasphemy is saying *no* to our life as it is,
saying *no* to our situation as impossible, hopeless,
saying *God* is not present here,
saying *God* does not have the power,
saying *Christ* may have redeemed the earth,
but it sure missed me and my situation.
Blasphemy is mocking *God*:
"*God* created my life and afterwards left,
saying, 'It's all very bad.'"

But we can say *yes* . . .
It's Etty's prayer [in the concentration camp],
"God, take me by Your hand;
I shall follow faithfully and not resist too much."
That's what Jesus meant when he said,
"Into thy hands I commend my spirit.
You and I, Father. We shall overcome."

We have the advantage over Jesus in our dying.
He's shown us the way of faith up to and in death.
And, too, we are sure *God* will be faithful to us
and present with us even as he was with Jesus.

This is the great promise:
possibility and hope in every situation,
even death.

The *Messiah* is come,
born again in our lives.
Therefore, life is always possible.
I can say *yes* to my life as it is
for *God* is with me.
The *Messiah* is here.
I wait for no other.

It Happens

Ever since *God* formed
the way life is,
the transforming *Jesus Christ event*
has been happening –
once and for all and ever again.

When it happens to me,
I experience reunion
with *God*
and Neighbor
and self.

When it happens to me,
my corrupted faith
is transformed into
radical faith:

faithful only
to the one, true *God,*
for the very good creation.

All this is
the quintessence
of gracious existence.

Trinitarian Epilogue

The *mysterious power* as *he, she,* or *it*
is heresy, making *God* an object,
making *God* in our own image.

Christian heresy is making Jesus *God.*
Jesus re-presents *God* but is not *God.*
We cannot swap faith for magic.

The *freedom* of Jesus, the *faith* of Jesus, and
his *passion* are our possibility:
to be as human as he was.

Yet, *Jesus the man's* not as historical
as the transforming *Christ the event* of
every person's existence.

Now the holy *spirit* Jesus promised is here,
always already at hand and always
coming to transform ev'rything.

The Historical Christ

I'm not as interested in the historical Jesus –
Objective facts that will not turn my life around –
As I am in tracing my life-changing journey
Through my hundreds of historic christ events.

The happenings of such events in my history
Burst illusion and heal deepest despair,
Saving me from the sin of separation from all,
Off'ring the word of acceptance, just as I am.

Many are the ways christ events transformed me:
Frank Laubach's presence impacted my youth;
JFK's death tore me apart in graduate school;
My first grandchild's birth deeply reunited me.

They come in personal and world-shaking ways,
In 9/11 and earth evolutionary ways,
In learning-to-deal-with-my-aging-body ways –
Bringing me to sight in my blindness, always.

In the beginning were universal christ events
Bringing creation to its knees and its greatness.
From everlasting to everlasting, and now,
They stand as the crux of our historical journeys.

Here's to the power that changes all!

~july 2006

III

from *Motivation for the Great Work: Forty Meaty Meditations for the Secular-Religious*

Why I Am Turned Off

I'm turned off by "John 3:16" at ball games,
By someone saying, "Only humans have rights!"
Or "All the Earth belongs to all!" usually meaning
Humans, at best, & the % of us with the most,
    at worst.

Why am I turned off by sexist language for *God*?
Choosing "he" or "she" seems we leave out "its,"
Obviously a bigger category than "she" and "he."
Speaking universally, we forget *God* loves
    everything.

Definitely "thou" is a more appropriate word,
Experiencing that she/he/it are *thou* and not *it*,
That is, if grace still happens and unites us with
"*God* above God," all beings, and with our very
    own selves.

Thanks be for the depth of spirituality,
Beyond religions and no-religion,
That keeps on happening the way it happens,
Verily, for the next 5 billion years and more.

The Universe Is Where I'm From

What's going on . . .
  the yearly cycle
  the seasonal cycle
  the monthly cycle
  the daily cycle
  sunrise
  sunset
  moon and stars shining
  clouds forming and moving
  dew, rain, snow, sleet, hail
  wind at all velocities
  smells of plants, flowers, and foliage
  sounds of birds and wind in the trees
  sight of mountains and oceans
  feeling of cold and heat
We know we are a part of the universe.

Fundamental gifts to humans from the universe:
  form
  breathing
  senses

brain power
reflecting
talking
singing
walking
dancing
will power
being loved
loving
being forgiven
forgiving
being cared for
caring

With these gifts we can build up or destroy . . .
our body
our mind
our spirit
our family
our organizations
our neighborhood
our town or city
our region
our nation
our united nations
our planet
our universe.

Spirit Does Not Promise

spirit does not promise . . .

> long life
> good health
> financial security
> a marriage that works
> loving children
> a nice house
> a solid job
> sweet dreams
> no pain
> a good education
> kind in-laws
> responsible government
> safe cities
> no taxes
> good neighbors
> and world peace

but *spirit* does promise . . .

> grace sufficient for every need
> forgiveness in spite of
> mercy without question
> peace that passes understanding
> balm for the deepest grief
> comfort for the greatest pain
> a calling whether we want it or not

purpose when we've lost our way
courage in spite of fear
more freedom than we can handle
refuge amid raging storms
rest for the weary
hope against hope
light in the darkest night
joy unspeakable
welcome home with open arms
resurrection in this life
love that will not let us go
its eternal presence

spirit does promise
all this abundant life,
but not as the world promises or giveth

and, believe it or not, *spirit* does promise
ways to end poverty, stop wars,
and save the earth

~printed in "The Catholic Northwest Progress," 11/22/01

The Prince of Darkness

Coming out of a friend's house into the dark
a good sized tree limb blind-sided me
    and brought blood.
I have a nice scab on my forehead as I write.
Yesterday I took my grandson Nolan's virus,
and has it been a whopper:
aching joints, pounding head, and swollen throat.
Dragging through the apartment with the fever
I bumped into a chair and broke my toe.
I went to the emergency room this morning –
my little toe on my right foot has turned indigo
    blue and is pointing to right field.
I sat in the hospital from 5:45 a.m. till 8:30,
    feverish, aching, and disgusted
    with the bureaucratic mess,
and waiting on the doctor to take his sweet time.

On the way out of the emergency room,
struggling up the steps to the parking lot,
I guess I looked like brokendownness itself,
hobbling in a new toeless shoe on my right foot,
carrying one shoe, wearing my eye patch,
sweaty and unshaven, mussed-up hair,
sporting a scab on my forehead, and muttering.

An old black man coming down the steps
looked me up and down and said,
"Ya know, suh, they can kill da body

but not da spirit, less you let 'em."

That stopped my world.
I looked round but he was gone.
I quit muttering, got in the car,
drove home with his words sounding in my deeps.
On the way Luther said, "The body they may kill.
'One little word shall fell' the Prince of Darkness
when he's standing on your neck
in charge of your consciousness."

The old man said that "one little word" to me today.
So, with *word* in hand,
I rose and beat hell out of the Prince of Darkness
and decided to try it again tomorrow
because it felt so good.

~june 2006

The Mystery of a Child

The presence of the Messiah is a mystery. . . . There is something surprising, unexpected about the appearance of salvation, something which contradicts pious opinions and intellectual demands. The mystery of salvation is the mystery of a child. . . . A child is real and not yet real, it is in history and not yet historical. Its nature is visible and invisible, it is here and not yet here. And just this is the character of salvation. Salvation has the nature of a child. . . . Only he who can see power in weakness, the whole in the fragment, . . . can say (with Simeon): Mine eyes have seen thy salvation. ~**Paul Tillich**, "Has the Messiah Come?" *The New Being*

Grandbaby Kaitlyn has mesmerized us
    since November 14th.
We see the miracle of her
    through father Jeremiah's countenance
    and announcement – "It's a girl!" –
    as he carried her out of the delivery room.
She is brand spanking new,
    filling us with wonder and awe.
She comes ready or not,
    forcing us to respond to her
    in all her utter vulnerability
    with our fumbling care.
She tries to see us who are loving her,
    but accepts our love blindly.
She does nothing useful;
    no one asks her what she does for a living.

She knows almost nothing;
     no one judges her for her lack of education.
She is sheer being,
     just there to be cared for and loved.
The miracle is that her "job" of just being
     transforms those around her:
     relatives that were alienated are reconciled;
     strangers become friends;
great-grandparents are rejuvenated;
     grumpies show compassion;
     judges show mercy.
Where did she learn to do all this?
She has mysterious power.
She must be a bit of being itself
     – like all God's children –
     bringing with her a bit of the new creation
          and new being.

The mystery of the messiah comes into our world
     anew in the birth of a baby,
          whoever it belongs to,
whatever gender, nationality, color, or religion.

It comes to us who think we do not want it or need it.
It comes to us hardened cynics who have given up
     on new life ever happening to us again.
It comes to us who think we have learned to live with
     separation and have given up on reunion.
It comes to us who have shunned religion;
     yet, it rattles us with deep spiritual rumblings.

It comes to us who are following every wise man
and every star, looking for that
which we will never find
and which was never promised.
The mystery of the messiah comes as it wills,
where it wills,
when it wills.
Sometimes it wills to come in the form of a child.

The Messiah has come.
Be ready or not for its coming again.

What a joy to me every time I am with her.
I have told Jeremiah, in a not unserious way,
    she is the greatest thing he has done till now,
        for she reconciles everything in her sphere.

~1995 Christmas letter

36

That I May Rise and Serve

That event, set off by that bullet
– by whomever –
turned me inside out
and changed my life forever.
Later, I learned the dynamics
of what was happening to me:

· an external event happens . . .
· occasioning interior crisis . . .
· sometimes opening me to reality . . .
· and leaving me great possibility . . .

to elect existence as it is given,
to make a new decision
to do what's necessary.

This event of the *mysterious power* comes to all
and leads to crisis, to truth, to new decision,
and new life.
It is so real we can hardly stand its power.
We call upon religious metaphor
to describe the terrible,
awful experience
that causes us to tremble
and yet brings new life.

Why is birth so excruciating?
John Donne* answers:

"Batter my heart . . .
to o'erthrow mee, and bend
Your force to breake, blow, burn,
   and make mee new. . . ."

And all for what? Donne says
the *great event* births in me *new life*
". . . That I may *rise*, and *stand*."
That I may rise and serve!

* Holy Sonnet XIV: "Batter My Heart, Three-Person'd God"

Gracious Freedom

Because of the gracious events in life
    and in my life

I am freed _from_ having to be saved
from the fear of failure
from the fear of death
from having to believe anything special
from finding meaning in anything I do
from finding meaning in any relationship
from having to go searching for love
from trying to be loveable
from having to do anything at all
from having to know anything at all
from having to be anything at all
from worrying what others think of me
       from securing my future
       from having to win
       from justifying my past
       from fulfilling my calling
from guilt
from anxiety
from sin
from having to be right
from having to be righteous
from being responsible to the world
from having to be myself
from trying to get to heaven
I am even _freed from_ having to be free.

I am freed _for_ loving *thee*
for loving *thy* creation
for obligation and responsibility
for creating the future
for fulfilling my destiny
for being my mystery
 depth
 and
 greatness
for reduplicating the deed
for following my bliss
for seizing my vocation
for being my happiness
for deciding and doing *thy* will
 for living in the ghettos
 for living among the poor

for cleaning the air and the rivers
 for helping the lame to walk
 and the blind to see

for telling the life-giving story
 for serving *thee*
 and *for* praising *thee* forever.

~january 1989

40

The Movement Needed

The movement needed is
    the intercommunion of creation.
But if the movement of those who care for the
    universe is not grounded in *spirit*, it will fail.
If grounded in *spirit*
    there will be no force great enough to stop it.
Who can stop a movement on which
    every being's life depends?
Who can stop a movement that is history long,
    universe wide, and *spirit* deep?
Who can stop a movement with
    a membership of all beings,
    all peoples, all cultures, all religions,
    and all sectors?
Who can stop a movement that's out
    to protect every being's home,
    every being's rights,
    and every being's best interests?
Who can stop a movement that is
    the big tent for all caring movements?

Be careful in trying to stop this movement.
Be enhanced by advancing it.
It's a movement whose time has come.
It's a movement worth body and soul.
This movement of *intercommunion*
    is the *great work*.

The *spirit*, the call, the story, the mandate
    – all these, and we,
    are creating this movement.

May we be so inspired . . .
    so motivated . . .
        and remotivated.

~printed in *The Ecozoic Reader,* Summer 2001, Vol. 1, No. 4

Radical Equality

As 20th century born I am not better
As a male I am not better
As the last of the Cock children I am not better
As a small town boy I am not better
As an educated person I am not better
As a Virginian I am not better
As a southerner I am not better
As an American I am not better
As a westerner I am not better
As a Caucasian I am not better
As a Christian I am not better
As a rich man I am not better
As a human I am not better
As an earthling I am not better
As a creature of our universe
    I am no better than any other
    creature in creation

IV

9/11 Poems

Emerging Peace?

my heart imploded
with the buildings
in New York and D.C.
and is buried now in grief
for our fallen innocents

I began to seethe
and want retaliation
because that's the way
I've been raised by my
eye-for-an-eye tribe

I could well understand
media and leaders
raised the same way
saying into the night
that America will

retaliate, get revenge,
no one gets by with this

we'll hunt 'em down
and erase the evil ones
from the face of the earth

but as I tried to sleep
with whirling images
these lines came to me
"if others are not at peace
then neither are we"

up came the question
how do we bring to peace
people of Libya and Sudan
Iraq and Afghanistan
Saddam and bin Laden

not by any military means
they will always find a way
to maim our body and soul
their commitment seems to be
much deeper than most

we are pushed to the wall
our military and defense
do not work like before
so let us fast and pray and
spend the zillions on peace

~september 12, 2001

On Their Behalf

eleven days later
a deluge of dialogue
has pushed me to account
for being an American

who am I to blame
those around the world
reflecting on their
love-hate for America

if they envy
our freedoms and good life
they seem to loathe
superpower ego

have we tyrannized
peoples and the planet
with maneuvers of greed
instead of global care

all in the name
of our national interests
have we justified
by whatever means

I am asked what
shape my repentance

will take for America's
terrorizing deeds

under the emerging truth
that we are one planet
and cannot tolerate
any terror at all

let this our tribute be
to those buried in NY and DC
that on their behalf
we stop the violence

on their behalf
we stop on earth
covert and overt terror
letting America go first

on their behalf
we pledge new allegiance
to *all* nations "under God
with liberty and justice for all"

"on their behalf". . .
a good idea or
that without which
none will survive?

~september 22, 2001

46

Global Dreaming

I had a dream the other night
about our needed plan
to save our world from terror
and unite our global band

as leader of the earth
I assigned all the leaders
of two-hundred plus nations
to gather and be readers

of their nations' lists
of heinous crimes against
humanity and the planet
for all to consense

listeners added to
each nation's awful list;
with "no rebuttal rule"
the readers did desist

Archbishop Tutu led each session
as he did in TRC days
pronouncing absolution on
those confessing apartheid

the leaders of the earth
then produced a ten-year plan

to care for all the planet
knowing they must and can

remembering the universe story
and the meaning of vocation
they took the global plan
to their respective nation

two-hundred national assemblies
heard the litany of crimes
and every last town meeting
built implementing schemes

to enact by next year's gathering —
on behalf of the population
and planetary species —
of Global Truth and Reconciliation

~september 24, 2001

Nonviolence

as I grieve over September 11
I fear for the future
remembering what happened
to Japan after Pearl Harbor
(3,457 killed, wounded, missing)
immediately and sometime later

though there was Doolittle's raid
on Tokyo within a few months
if Oppenheimer had been ready
there would have been bombs
that will live in infamy
dropped then instead of four years later

first on Hiroshima, August 6, 1945,
(130,000 killed, wounded, missing)
days later on Nagasaki, August 9, 1945,
(75,000 killed, wounded, missing)
I wonder about Gandhi's response
to all the sophisticated killings

I must read what he wrote in his diary
and if our bombs had something to do
with his reaching out to the Muslims
for he died January 30, 1948
from a fanatical Hindu's bullet
because "Gandhi is a Muslim-lover"

I also wonder what history
will say was the best policy
sophisticated killings or nonviolence
that freed India through fasts
freed Poland through strikes
and freed Americans through sit-ins

not very sophisticated
but very (what is the right word)
civilized or evolved or . . . or
respectful of the enemy
assuming their take on good and evil
is not absolutely wrong

~september 25, 2001 (published in *Poets Against War*)

Sic Semper Tyrannus

when i am tyrannized by massa
i sometimes hear the truth and overcome
when i am tyrannized by the future
i sometimes hear the truth and overcome
when i am tyrannized by crucifiers
i pray to hear the truth and overcome
à la jesus' deciding no one takes my life from me
'cause i freely give it
at such times tyranny is overcome

when i am tyrannized by hitler

i hear the truth and try to kill him
on behalf of 6 million jews & future generations
à la bonhoeffer who prayed
not to be tyrannized by a nazi hanging

à la rosa parks on the bus
who prayed not to be tyrannized by white
    alabamians
à la gandhi who prayed
not to be tyrannized by englishmen and
    religious fundamentalists

does this make any sense
is this in some testament
yes in the testament of life
tyranny is overcome
thank you jesus dietrich rosa and gandhigi
we shall overcome
freedom is as freedom does
or is it freedom does as freedom is

and what about the tyrants
sometimes we have to put a foot on their necks
and a spear to their hearts
as on my virginia flag
saying *sic simper tyrannus*: thus always to tyrants
but sometimes we let them up
if we think they finally understand

~september 27, 2001

51

V

from *Our Universal Spirit Journey: Reflection & Verse for Creation's Sake*

Where I'm Coming From

Spirit is the inner dimension of everything.
It is "always already" present,
For creation is transparent to *spirit.*
It is the dynamic of communion within creation,
Sustaining, wakening, forming, engaging, uniting.
Spirit is making all things new.

It founds but transcends religions and cultures.
Spirit is our primal universal symbol.
All are spiritual, being on *its* immense journey.
The *spirit* movement abounds.
Deny, resist, or respond to *its* call,
Never doubt it eternally sounds.

Traditional *Spirit* Words

Whither shall I go from *spirit* – *it* is always here
spirit was, is, and ever shall be
spirit loves and gives *itself* to and for the world
all are sons and daughters of *spirit*:
      the stars, mountains, and creatures
spirit promises and gives abundant life to those
      who are aware of *its* presence
the wind of *spirit* blows where *it* will
spirit is reconciling the world
spirit dwells among us, full of glory
spirit is making all things new, rough places plain,
      and crooked ways straight
spirit is like a refiner's fire
spirit is the way, the truth, and the life
no one comes to fulfillment except by *spirit*
spirit is all about sacrificial love
spirit is resurrection power
spirit is always coming again
spirit never leaves us comfortless
spirit is where two or three are gathered in *its* name
great things will the children of *spirit* do
spirit is the be-all and end-all

Till All Breath Is Gone

We got Enlightened
descended Mt. Myth
to the Promised (flat) Land
where there was fact and
human progress instead
of milk and honey.

Thousands, hundreds of years
to climb the mountain
only tens to come down
for decline is faster
than ascent; throwing
out stories faster

Than creating great myths.
who's to say which is
better: mountain, flatland?
both are illusion –
the one otherworldly
the other immortal
empiricism.

Whether heavenly or
this-worldly progress
we are left in limbo
for our lives are about
seeing through to the mean-
ing of birth and breath

Not chasing promises
that someday will come
in the sweet-by-and-by
or at retirement –
given new gold watches
to wind going home.

So promise us some height
some depth and substance
right now, downtown Flatland.
we know we're not
el cap'tans of our fate
so let's deeply breathe.

Let us have a go at
our interiors –
everlovin' moments
experiencing
wonder and fulfillment
till all breath is gone.

'Tis

<u>Ancient</u>: all in *spir-it*
<u>Buddhism</u>: consciousness of *spir-it*
<u>Christianity</u>: transparency to *spir-it*
<u>Hinduism</u>: oneness with *spir-it*
<u>Islam</u>: allegiance to *spir-it*
<u>Judaism</u>: awesomeness of *spir-it*
<u>Sufism</u>: children of *spir-it*
<u>Taoism</u>: manifestation of *spir-it*

alphabetically,
all my religions tell me
who I am

spir-it creature

we are
spir-it creatures
created by *it*
transparent to *it*
reflecting *it*
creating with *it*

seamlessly
at one
with *it*
eternally
graciously
and
anxiously

56

so let us be
who we are

thankfully
embracing
embodying
announcing
the fact
of our lives

spir-it is

'Tis

Spirit Makes the World Go Round

Cabaret says *money* makes the world go round
politicians say *power* makes the world go round
Hollywood says *they* make the world go round
education says *knowledge* makes the world go round
religion says *belief* makes the world go round

but *spirit* makes the world go round

for *spirit* encounters the big and small
the rich and the poor
the educated and illiterate
the believing and unbelieving

why
to make us all grateful
for the way life is
even when we ain't got no
      money
      power
      entertainment
      knowledge
        or
      belief

Spiritually Correct

Does it matter
what we call *it*
so long as we unite

Whether we call *it*
> *Spirit*
> *God*
> *One*
> *Ultimate*
> *Numinous*
> *Father*
> *Goddess*
> *Emptiness*

we bow before mysterious power
blowing this way and that
sometimes at our back
sometimes in our faces
but always stirring
whether we sense it or not

Words are hardly the message
only a medium of expression
of what we perceive
> images
> poetry
> metaphor

our way . . .

to say something
about what we see
intuit
experience

Our words are not *it*
even holy writ
only inklings
and intimations

The message is always
written on the wind
sometimes in-
spiring the heart

Therefore,
to be
spiritually correct
unite in
its presence

Spirituality

spirituality reflects *spirit* in the pool
of one's inner life
spirituality reflects *spirit* in the prism
of one's outer life

Simply

We do not have to believe in some deity
    to live spiritually.
In fact, belief often clouds our seeing.

Simply, if we see in

...the chewing of food the wonder of taste
...our associations the wonder of being together
...the meteor shower the wonder of the cosmos
...our grandchildren the wonder of their wonder
...9/11 events the wonder of our precious finitude
...dreaming the wonder of imagination
...sexuality the wonder of attraction and union
...birth and death the wonder of life

then we begin to get it,
this thing called spirituality,
the way of life that is intercommunion,
for all created subjects
given to see to the heart of what is.

Simply, spirituality is for all and everyone.

    ~may 2006

Where Does *Spirit* Fit In?

King Sisyphus ended up in Hades
to eternally roll a huge rock up a long, steep hill,
only to watch it roll back down the same side.
For him demands are unending, thankless,
and end in unsuccessful efforts.
He might well have said, "This is not fair."
Or, "The gods are against me."
Or, "What's the use?"
For Sisyphus life is hell to live.
Where is *spirit*? Just over the hill?

King Tantalus, another king offending the gods,
also paid the price in Hades.
He was condemned to stand beneath fruit-laden
boughs, up to his chin in water.
Whenever he bent his head to drink,
the water receded,
and whenever he reached for the fruit,
the branches moved beyond his grasp.
Thus to "tantalize" is to tease or torment
by offering something desirable
but keeping it out of reach.
For Tantalus, too, life is hell to live.
Where is *spirit*? Just out of reach?

Rich Man had much land, many crops, and
decided to build bigger barns to store his goods.
"When my barns are full I will celebrate," he said.

Anxious about the future he was not merry yet.
Jesus said God called Rich Man a fool. Why?
Was it because he would build ever more barns?
Or that his life was under siege by the future?
Or that he spent his life, now, securing the future?
In any case, Rich Man's life was spent –
that night he died.
Where is *spirit*? With more riches?

Faust wanted a monument erected in his name.
Aging, he heard clanking outside his window.
Were they completing his monument, finally?
No, they were digging his grave.
Life was about consecrating his knowing and doing.
Was Faust a fool for wanting his name live forever?
Where is *spirit*? In our great accomplishments?

All these fools were from the more distant past.
Are there any alive in our day?
There's **Lester** (Kevin Spacey) of *American Beauty*,
a pitiful, middle-aged man.
Was he redeemed when he got freed up
and did what felt good no matter whom it hurt?
The smile on his face toward his tragic end
was hardly the smile of one who has come through.
Like Faust, he was caught up in his ego needs.
Where is *spirit*? In selfish lust for freedom?

And **Melvin** (Jack Nicholson) in *As Good As It Gets*.
He flaunted his neuroses all over Manhattan:

hating dogs, gays, women, Jews — and himself.
But he became attached to the little dog,
befriended his gay neighbor,
fell in love with his waitress (Helen Hunt),
and paid the doctor to cure her son.
Melvin and *Carol* got awakened, event after event,
until they began to see that their lives
were as good as they were going to get.
Where is *spirit*? In the little big events of life?

Life is Beautiful, with Roberto Benigni as *Guido*,
is another movie that won many Oscars.
It too is about a man who bumps into creation
and finds a wife and a son to love.
This outrageous man proclaims life is good,
even in a Nazi death camp in Italy,
in one masquerade after another to save his son.
For Guido, all of life is a stage.
Where is *spirit*? In the role one is given to play?

Don't forget *Erin Brockovich* (Julia Roberts),
a fool whose life and family were coming apart
when a legal case-and-a-half bumped into her:
contaminated water runoff from the PG&E plant.
She helped prove they were knowingly liable
to tens of families living nearby.
This woman's passion rose in relation to
the compassion she felt for the victims.
She became their champion and PG&E's nightmare.
Look what she can do when motivated.

Where is *spirit*? Born of compassion?

An older Oscar winner, **Zorba** (Anthony Quinn),
who like Faust wanted to build a monument.
His was a conveyor from the mine down the hill
to the coast for the minerals to be shipped.
Trestles and railway installed,
they cut the ribbon on the first run.
Vibrations of wagons set off total collapse.
It fell apart and piled onto the ground.
End of a dream and Zorba broke down and cried?
Hardly. He began the dance he's famous for –
a more fitting monument.
Where is *spirit*? In the celebration of real life?

Victor Frankl saw and reflected on how fellow
Jewish prisoners dealt with Nazi death camps.
Their undying spirits amazed and changed him.
Many trusted the Sun would come up tomorrow
or the memory of the *thou* of a loved one.
At another camp was **Elly Hillesum**,
a saint as she prepared to go to the gas chamber.
Among her last words:
"I vow to live my life out there to the full."
Where is *spirit*? In any conceivable situation?

And **Gandhi**, a different kind of lawyer,
confounding the government of South Africa
on behalf of all "colored,"
and liberating his homeland from British rule.

His nonviolent ideology and movement
touched the life of young **Martin Luther King, Jr.,**
as they brought the Birmingham system to heel,
and helped change the laws of their homeland.
Where is *spirit*? Hiding in social injustices?

Likewise, **Desmond Tutu** of South Africa,
who helped conceive the most daring
secular forgiveness structure of our time:
the Truth and Reconciliation Commission,
wherein some 21,000 victims of apartheid
gave testimony, and over 7000 perpetrators
confessed and sought forgiveness.
Thousands were changed by forgiveness.
A model honoring a deeper law than on the books
has spread around the world.
Where is *spirit*? In forgiveness and reconciliation?

And a favorite colleague from Pune, India,
Shakuntalah Belge Jadhav,
whom I met when she was nineteen-years-old,
taking human development programs
across the State of Maharashtra.
She has spent her last twenty-some years
living with and training thousands of villagers
to pick up their villages and their lives.
She is now sick with cancer
but has not stopped her great work.
Where is *spirit*? In spending self on behalf of others?

Thomas Berry, now eighty-seven years of age,
is spending his life caring for creation.
His witness through his teaching and books
has brought us a new vision for the earth,
a new picture of the universe,
a new role for the human,
and a definition of *the great work* awaiting us:
mutual care by all for all.
As I write he is preparing another book.
Where is *spirit*? In loving creation?

Human stories show us how *spirit* fits our lives.

"Where is *spirit*?"

·Just over the hill?
·Just out of reach?
·With more riches?
·In our great accomplishments?
·In selfish lusts for freedom?
·In the little big events of life?
·In the role one is given to enact?
·Born of compassion?
·In the celebration of life and death?
·In any conceivable situation?
·Hiding in the social injustices of our time?
·In social forgiveness and reconciliation?
·In expending oneself on behalf of others?
·In loving creation?

Our answer to Where is *spirit*?
makes the difference to the way we live our lives.
If our life stories reveal *spirit* is present,
then it's a matter of how we bow to *it*.

"*Spirit*" Etymology

spirit . . .
is the heart of creation; *it*
    never stops creating
    dynamizes process
    ennobles existence
    lets loose grace
    births holiness

creation . . .
is a piece of work; it
    never stops creating
    is in process
    is good
    is gracious
    is holy

life . . .
is a piece of creation; it
    never stops creating
    is in process
    is good

is gracious
is holy

almost seems natural
to love life
and all creation

since *spirit*
transpires
and inspires

such is the history
of this word *spiritus*
'a fine wind blowing'

Is *Spirit* Real?

Which is more real . . .

birth of my sons or death of my parents?
love of peace or fear of war?
scientific fact or theoretical concept?
poetic image or meticulous description?
truth or illusion?
experience or intuition?
risk or security?
event or story?
faith or miracle?

Which is less real . . .

proof or ambiguity?
commitment or detachment?
feeling or calculation?
decision or intention?
vision or plan?
subjectivity or objectivity?
light or dark?
belief or fantasy?
feast or famine?
doubt or certainty?
laughter or tears?

Which is really real . . .

mental image or photograph?
inclusiveness or exclusiveness?
childhood or age?
a rose or a thorn?
chocolates or fasting?
a kiss or a snub?
consciousness or unconsciousness?
time or space?
past or future?
sound or silence?
dream or actuality?

When was the last time
I experienced something real?

Have I experienced . . .

beginning and ending?
fullness and emptiness?
memory and being present?
sadness and joy?
intimacy and wonder?
boredom and mission?
fear and comfort?
power and weakness?

Have I experienced . . .

despair and tranquility?
pain and pleasure?
estrangement and reunion?
it-ness and thou-ness?
forgiveness and separation?
dread and hope?
heart and soul?
greatness and depth?

Have I experienced . . .

closed down and opened up?
freedom and imprisonment?
dead right and dead wrong?
imagination and vacuity?
dead end and new life?
last chance and second chance?

71

raging storm and gentle breeze?
twilight and dawn?
mystery and awe?

Has *spirit* happened to me in the midst of these?
What is real?
What have I experienced?

The Way *Spirit* Works

The way *spirit* works
   is not the way
   the tradition says:
A power from outside this world enters it
   and makes something happen.
That is otherworldly magic,
   which went out of vogue some time ago.
Spirit is always *of* and *for* this world — and *by*?
I guess *it* comes from the same place
   everything else comes from.

Son John received this e-mail
   from a friend in Indonesia:

   *"rella gave birth last night: aruna francisca, 44
   cm, 2.25 kg. . . . it was pretty amazing this morn-
   ing to hold her in my arms. i looked up at the sky
   last night while waiting, and i was wondering*

if there was anything up there besides green
-house gases. looking at her little face was like
seeing the universe and knowing that it is good.
                ~regards, jiway"

At such awesome moments
        of "looking at her little face,"
We create words like "wonder" and awesome."
We may look to the heavens, but we know
        where these phenomena come from —
"Like seeing the universe" reveal its heart
        and "knowing that it is good."
Gracious moments give us a peek
        at the way *spirit* works.

Eternal Now

                what is
                reveals itself
                continually
                for me
                to see

                i see
                with open eyes
                joyful heart
                grateful
                to be

Bet You've Experienced It

The meaning of "the happening of transparency?"
    Let the poetry answer . . .

I saw the light
blind but now I see
been to the mountain
happy day
the be-all and end-all
turning point
it all came together
alignment
in the zone
meaning bleeding from every moment
new vision
epiphany
sacred moment
inspired
transformed
transfixed
this is the time
this is the place
rang my chime
red alert
advent
cataclysmic
defining moment
before and after
dead man walking

scales falling from my eyes
bowled over
great god a'mighty, free at last
synchronicity
gestalt
eureka
aha
wow
overwhelmed
assaulted
awesome encounter
terrifying
blown apart
life-changing
kairotic
resurrected
grace
took off my shoes
holy ground
at the center
called
I'm the one
we're it
the Hesperides
kingdom come on earth
strange peace
miraculous
the great event

. . . like songwriters, we sometimes "see through" . . .

what a wonderful world
zipadeedooda
my or my, what a wonderful day
goodness gracious, great balls of fire
lightning moment, blazing spark
the lightning of the terrible swift sword
I'm going to Graceland
I know what I know
lost in a sweet place
all is well
I surrender
celebrate
wade in the water
I found you just in time
everything is satisfaction
it's a grand night for singing
the earth is aglow
never saw things going so right
there's wonder in most everything I see
does enchantment pour out of every door
there's nowhere on earth that I would rather be
I could have danced all night
my heart took flight
oh what a beautiful morning
all the sounds of the earth are like music
on a clear day how it will astound you
that the glow of your being outshines every star
you can see forever and ever and evermore
the trumpets of glory now call me to ride
whithersoever they blow, onward to glory I go

. . . sometimes these common, popular words
make sense when we experience the
      primal
      life-changing
      secular-religious
      other-world-in-this-world
events of life. . . .

"Transparency?" Yeah, we've experienced it.

Sometimes . . .

During transparent encounters
we go through some such sloop:

      focusing
      reflecting
      interpreting
      internalizing
      resolving
      symbolizing
      embodying
      letting loose

leaving us to have or reject existence/creation
    good as given,
and bringing us to sing with Louis
    "What a wonderful world!"

Heart of Creation

from the heart of creation
whether it be
dinosaur or the latest e-

vent invading consciousness
whether it be
a birth or catastrophe

spirit is happening
whether it be
now or then in eternity

Here and Now

Not only do we live in the second-story
if we think that one day after we die
we will go to another world,
or that we came from another world,
or that there is a something up there, out there,
or back there that is finally in charge of life;
but also we live in the second-story
if we think there is *spirit* out there
that we will one day grasp
if we keep on the right path.
Second-story reality denies *spirit* here and now,
denies that there is only one world of reality,
and that this is it.

We are not preparing to live;
we are living now
at whatever age
or in whatever condition.
The kingdom is now, eternally.
Reality is present, here, at hand;
there is only one reality
and *spirit* is its heart.

The life question is "What's happening?"
followed by "How do I fit in?"
Spirit shouts and whispers, "Let go! Follow Me!"
changing all *it* encounters.

Thus, to talk about *spirit*, we talk about now,
not the sweet-by-and-by of some ideal future,
when we finally enter a perfect state.

There is no 2-, 4-, 6-, 8-step spirit journey.
Just our responses to what's happening:
whether or not we give ourselves
to *spirit's* awesome lead.

Spirit is going on in our lives.
We can leap into *it*,
shut down and flat-line,
or do a lifelong search for *it*.
Two of the three are illusions.

Spirit is always
erupting,
creating,
sanctifying,
    and
whispering,
    "Here and Now!"
    "Here and Now!"
ad infinitum.

Epiphany

creation's
spirit heart
is beating

spirit's good
all is good
life is good

spirit's no-
where if not
everywhere

celebrate
"*spirit's* here!"
this season

Meeting

if the meeting is the thing
between *spirit* and me
I'm glad we are two
with eventful dialogue

if we were one
we couldn't meet
so I promise to be
on time and present

'cause maybe it's me
missing the meetings
if *spirit's* always present
and never once late

a big meeting past
when assassinations
flipped my universe
and my life's direction

or a little meeting today
when granddaughter
penned 'I LOV YU'
for her first sentence

I'll look and listen
through such events
for the meeting next
between thou and me

for these meetings
illumine my life
making the mundane
holy comm-union

"let's continue to meet
on the sly or
in broad daylight
again and every now"

Meaning

more stuff gives meaning
entertainment gives meaning
long life gives meaning

they say
no

they say
thanks for life the way it is gives meaning
giving life where it isn't gives meaning

they say
don't go to school to find meaning
don't get rich to find meaning

they say
the meaning of life is to expend it
expend it before the age of 33 and after

they say
you mess up
trying to save it

who are they anyway
and how'd they figure out what to say

Happy Birthday, Thomas

Billions of years ago
more or less
you began with a bang
and ever since
you've been evolving

You've had a home
on Earth
in the universe
with one humongous family
of kindred spirits
from butterflies to Teilhard
brothers and sisters all

You've been sustained
even loved
by what has been
is now
and is ever coming

Think about
the next phase
of your journey
in peace
flow like the river
toward the tranquil sea
and crashing waves

Fear not
lest you be forgotten
for you have been
are and will always be
a blessed member
of this intercommunion

That keeps creating
transforming
eternally
that has no place to go
save *spirit* is
already there

~for Thomas Berry's 87th Birthday
november 9, 2001

You Want to See Happiness?

When have I experienced . . .
The Kingdom of Heaven?
The kairotic moment?
When have my *yeses* to life transformed it?

When like Buddha have I awakened to see the
    morning star?
When like Jesus have I made the speech to Pilot
    and experienced being at one with *the mystery*?

When like Francis have I cared enough to
    kiss a leper?
When like Alyosha have I fallen down to
    kiss the earth and risen a man?
When like Meursault have I understood
    not "living like a dead man"?
When have I really wanted the life I really have?

When have I experienced . . .
The strange happiness of Sisyphus?
Curly's "one thing"?
Camus' "embracing the implacable grandeur
    of this life"?
e.e.'s "everything which is natural which is
    infinite which is 'Yes'"?
Kaz's living unhappiness as happiness?

Fulfillment is embodying happiness
    with all the happy and saying,
"You want to see happiness, look at us!"

    Blessed are the happy,
    for they grasp the power to say *yes*.
    Selah.

        ~june 2006

Happy Death

Francis, Gandhiji, Albert, and Martin,
Joseph, Kaye, Lyn, and Liza,
Virginia, Margaret, and Mama Dotte —
they lived and died the happy death
and showed what I can do

In their lives headed toward death
brother death became
their lively, eternal guide
(hardly the last enemy)
their sanction of life
making it holier

Of course they feared
yes they were in pain
yet death did not hold them captive
he was their gracious friend
not the darkness
but the one who lit the way

They breathed the *yes*
that to live or to die
is to live eternally
happy

O to live the happy death
Selah

For Elizabeth*

Spirit is always home,
In life or death or beyond,
If we have the eyes to see.
The promise, *spirit* is with us;
The truth, *spirit* is with us;
The power, *spirit* is with us.

Victory is ours through *spirit*.
Nothing in death nor life,
In this world nor any other,
In the universe high or low,
Nothing in all creation
Can separate us from *spirit*.

We come from *spirit*,
We live with *spirit*,
We return to *spirit*.
We are thy children,
Always at home.
Blessed be thy name forever.

We sometimes stay home,
Sometimes walk alone,
Later to return home,
Met with open arms
And great celebration,
For we are thy children.

We come from *spirit*,
We go with *spirit*,
We return to *spirit* –
Never far away,
Always already present.
Blessed be thy name forever.

We live eternally,
Past, present, and future:
In *spirit* eternal before,
In *spirit* eternal now,
In *spirit* eternal hereafter.
Blessed be thy name forever.

We come from *spirit*,
We live with *spirit*,
We return to *spirit*.
We give thee back thine own.
Give her thy eternal rest,
Enfold her in thy arms forever.

In thy eternal peace
Hold her dear.
She belongs to thee.

Hallowed be thy name.
Thine is the kingdom,
The power, and the glory
        forever.

* for Elizabeth Williams, who died much too young

90

How Sense Emerged

Was it the awe
and the wonder
amid the flare
and the heat?

Was it the awe
and the beauty
amid the sound
and the beat?

Was it the awe
of communion
amid the fear
of defeat?

Was it allure
and attraction
amid the dark
of the night?

Was it the tug
of reunion
amid the sun's
warming light?

How sense emerged —
its origin?
Aye, it came
by *spirit's* might.

All Things Created Equal*

fish outswim humans
rabbits outhop humans
squirrels outclimb humans
birds outfly humans
horses outrun humans
bees outpollinate humans
viruses outmaneuver humans
rocks outmeditate humans
weather outsmarts humans
sun outshines humans
earth outmothers humans
life outlasts humans
spirit outmercies humans

are humans created equal to all things?
no and yes

---

* As Thomas Berry says in a letter to a magazine editor (*What Is Enlightenment*, Fall/Winter 2001, p. 13), "all elements of creation are not equal quantitatively as objects, but are equal qualitatively as subjects.... This comprehensive community is the supreme value, not simply the human community."

Toward Intereverything

from separatism to interbeing
from naturalism to intercreation
from environmentalism to interuniverse

from nationalism to internation
from tribalism to intercommunity
from classism to interequality

from humanism to interreality
from intellectualism to interrationality
from scientism to interknowledge

from capitalism to intereconomy
from socialism to interwellbeing
from consumerism to intersimplicity

from fanaticism to interdependence
from liberalism to intercompassion
from conservatism to interpreservation

from fundamentalism to interreligious
from secularism to intertransparency
from spiritualism to interspirituality

   don't scoff at the awkward words
   just move on out to the inter-
   communion of all things
   knowing all is one

By Cosmic Design?

At Timberlake watching young people
gape as they hear Thomas say
the U.S. Constitution is destructive,
declaring only human rights;
or hearing him ask
now that western civilization
has passed through its religious
and humanist phases,
What next?

On the way forward from our past,
this cosmological age
highlights awesome seasons
that birth rituals
and daily sunrises and sunsets
that spiritize existence,
sanctifying early mornings
with meditation
and late evenings
with reverie:
    parents reading to and
    cuddling with their children,
    answering big questions,
    rubbing backs and humming
    as the little ones slip into
    earth's dark, sacred night

Are we not spiritual
    by cosmic design
and for cosmic reason?

Go Fly

go fly with Stephen Hawking

we will mount our wheelchairs
decked out with mega voice
with his smile and wit
flying his cosmology
far out, deep, and wide

we will get perspective
on where we came from
and where we go
relearning our name
and place

"Who am I" is a massive think
with the deepest feel
of "what be I"
and mighty resolve
of "what do I"

I am "who I am" in the universe
so let me, myself, and I
go fly
and come back to earth
I-mazed

Nature Teaches Us

We learn . . .
>awe through lightning
>beauty through flowers
>majesty through mountains
>fear through thunder
>leadership from geese
>teamwork from ants
>parenting from elephants
>visioning from eagles
>maneuvering from viruses
>communication from dolphins

We learn . . .
>love through offsprings
>forgiveness from dogs
>community from bees
>ingenuity from beavers
>tenacity from squirrels
>sacrifice from crops
>wonder through spiderwebs
>contentment from cows
>curiosity from cats
>play from monkeys

We learn . . .
>warmth from sun
>hard work from mules
>direction from waterways

force from hurricanes
mystery through night skies
power from wind
cleansing through rain
transformation from caterpillars
peace through snow

We learn . . .
extinction from dinosaurs
risk through planting
calm from trees
praise from birds
endurance from camels
terror through fires
endlessness through waves
relaxation from bears
finitude through earthquakes
defense through predators

We learn . . .
dying from Fall
death from Winter
resurrection from Spring
nourishment from Summer
interdependence through eating
union through breeding
connectedness through vistas
dependence through breathing
reflection through night
anticipation through dawn

We learn . . .
> the reverence of intercommunion
> seeing *spirit*
> through
> nature's transparent veil.

One Big Free Lunch

Consider what's free.
Birth: here I am, free.
Breath: every breath I take, free.
Sight: every sight I see, free.
Every sound I hear, free.
Every thought, prayer, decision, act, FREE.
On and on: dirt, food, bacteria, nerve endings, imagination,
sensuality, creativity, family, calling, grace . . . all FREE.
Our life in this universe really is one big free lunch.

Catechetical question:
> What is the chief end of us creatures?
Absolutely obvious answer:
> To give thanks without ceasing . . .
>> which is also free
>> and the natural therapy.
What a universe!

~november, 2005

Note: Thanksgiving Day began 13.7 billion years ago, not in 1621.

Uni-verse

her pulse rate beeps and flashes
as she lies post-surgery
aping body universe

> one beat
> one heart
> one life

beating out her rhythm
in the citadel of time
from the beginning till now

> one beat
> one heart
> one life

humans we are not except
as universal beings
in the planetary rite

> one beat
> one heart
> one life

> gi-ven
> for all
> *en masse*

~TCC Hospital, Galax, VA

"Just Do It" Can't Do It Alone

Out of nothing comes something every time.
That's the way it is, *just watch it.*
Out of cosmic crisis came the air we breathe;
Out of slavery comes freedom;
Out of death comes life.
That's the way it is, *just trust it.*

Out of terrorism will come global unity.
That's the way it is, *just weave it.*
Out of poverty will come equity;
Out of AIDS will come global health;
Out of biocide will come planetary care.
That's the way it is, *just seed it.*

Out of powerlessness comes power, every time.
That's the way it is, *just free it.*
Spirit brings something out of nothing,
Not by a zap but sacrifice —
Some being's offering that changes things.
That's the way it is, *just give it.*

> *"Just do it"*
> can't do it
> alone.

Journeyed

As a proud human being
I tell myself I am
in charge of my journey.
Like pilgrims of yore
I do spiritual practices
and journey spiritual paths
that lead on the way
to the mountain top
and to perfection.

But when I look back on my life
I see I have been journeyed
by that which journeys all.
In each encounter
I experience beatitudes
of the awesome way:
reflection
interpretation
and thanksgiving.

As a "theologian"* said
in a better moment:
> "If it took *all that*
> to bring me to *this moment*,
> I wouldn't change a thing."

———
* Marilyn Monroe

Gifts of the *Spirit*

Tell me why there is something and not nothing
Tell me why something comes from no-thing

Tell me why some things are better than others
      Such as

        Being is better than not being
        Mystery is better than knowledge
        Consciousness is better than stupor
        Grace is better than achievement
        Communion is better than separation
        Faith is better than beliefs
        Freedom is better than bondage
        Mercy is better than law
        Love is better than hate
        Care is better than care less
        Vocation is better than work
        Community is better than self-centered
        Peace is better than war
        Fulfillment is better than rewards
        Happiness is better than existing

Tell me why these are quality-of-life things
      heart desires
Not things to consume, store, and throw away

But really tell me why real things in life are gifts
      and the rest we have to buy

We Are Spiritual Beings
created . . .

*

* * *

*

to *see*
to *care*
to *be* aware
to *live* simply
to *love* creation
to *work* on behalf of
to *celebrate* our living
to *reflect* on the awesome
to *serve* the shattered earth
to *dream* the impossible dream
to *home* on earth as one community

=

=

I Bow To *Spirit*: *Namaste*

Through you
I bow to *spirit*.
Namaste.

Whether you believe the "trinity,"
or "spirit" as the name for all three,

you believe *it* is,
from the beginning till now,
creating, recreating.
Namaste.

Spirit works *its* own way
everyday through events,
spoken, written, or imaged word;
through any part of creation,
through any person,
or through a vision:
spirit truths and lifes us.
Namaste.

Spirit is breath and non-,
height and depth,
edge and center,
beginning and end,
non-being in being.
Namaste.

Born of *spirit*.
In *spirit* we live, move,
and have our being.
Blessed be we by *spirit*.
Namaste.

So bow to all others in *its* name,
Its children all.
Namaste.

104

Spiritually Evolved?

As we evolve do we get better?
Are molecules better than atoms?
Or multicellular better than cellular?
Or bigger-brained better than smaller-?

Are things better than ever?
What about the tens of million humans
and thousands of species
we killed during the 20th century?
Which century is more evolved,
the last one or the first of the first millennium?

What does evolution have to do with *spirit*?
Does *spirit* evolve?
Do the evolved become more spiritual?
How can anything be any closer
to *spirit* than anything else,
regardless of time and space?

Who is more enlightened?
is a different question.
Can a group of humans
come together and care
for the masses,
    the biosphere,
    the geosphere,
    and the atmosphere?

If so, are they more evolved?
Yes.

More aware of *spirit's* presence?
Maybe.

Any closer to *spirit*?
How can they be?

Any better?
Of course not,
for *spirit* is impartial
(or absolutely partial
to everything).

VI

from *At One With the Heart of Creation: Reflections and Verse on the Spirit Journey*

Spirit Journey

spirit is . . .
   always happening to us on *its* journey
   always reconciling us to *its* oneness
   always awakening us to *its* mystery
   always enlightening us with *its* presence
   always freeing us for *its* mission
   always calling us to *its* great work
   always fulfilling us in *its* abundance
   always creating us by *its* power
   always sustaining us on *its* way
   always transforming us in *its* image
   always reigning over us by *its* grace
       therefore . . .
           all is one
           all is whole
           all is good
           all is blessed

Lift My Spirit

I sit and wait for a movie to lift my spirit,
for it to prick and explode my illusions
and to leave me with a vision of new creation.

It surely doesn't have to be a box office hit,
so violent and gruesome I scrunch in my seat,
nor so freaky or maudlin that I want to leave.

It doesn't have to have famous stars or director,
sensational stage craft or outlandish price tag,
nor a blitz of TV ads coming at me for weeks.

Rabbit Proof Fence, Winged Migration, Whale Rider
lifted my spirit as sisters escaped the whites,
a species of nature soared, and a tribe was reborn.

The Pianist uplifted me with his spirit,
surviving the devastations of war in his Poland
where once he was the artist of a dying order.

So you see, it doesn't take much to lift my spirit,
just a hour or two of a story of great life journey
responding to *spirit* from the heart of creation.

That Which Wakes All

I'm not sure who woke up whom
this morning, the birds or I,
but awake we both are, sure
that there's something to wake up to

Their kingdom and mine are one
as we listen to and watch
each other's kindred spirit,
sensing there's that which wakes us all

O That Which Is

Oh that which sees via my seeing
       that tastes via my tasting
       that touches via my touching
       that hears via my hearing
Oh that which speaks via my speaking
       that sings via my singing
       that laughs via my laughing
       that cries via my crying
Oh that which dreams via my dreaming
       that creates via my creating
       that prays via my praying
       that rejoices via my rejoicing

Oh that which breathes via my breathing
    that communes via my communing
    that loves via my loving
    that serves via my serving

Oh that which exists
    via the heart of my being
    is surely more
    via the heart of all being

Christmas

Why celebrate Christmas
why such a hullabaloo
she asked good questions I said
but what answer will she listen to

    Life is full of wonder
    full of love and joy and peace
    full of hope and communion
    of possibility openness

    You and I've experienced
    such gifts many times and more
    bringing meaning to our lives
    filling full what seemed empty before

Remember all the times
in spite of doubt we could not
give into the lie of lies
that living is just a senseless plot

Life's what we celebrate
at Christmas the very ground
of meaning purpose and love
not despair and hopelessness abound

She said I've got it now
ev'ry tiny baby's birth
regardless whose when or where
reveals the story of sacred worth

Yes life is so very good I said

Easter

Then she asked about Easter
the great Christian centerpiece
what about eternal life
I cannot make sense of that can you

    It is hard to explain I said
    that life is resurrection
    seeds shooting up from the earth
    butterfly winging from its prison

    about metamorphosing
    apartheid-ers forgiven
    Berlin walls tumble-ing down
    species from extinction's grave risen

    being born a second time
    new heart beating in my breast
    scales falling from my eyes
    blind but seeing life anew and yes

    miracles of reunion
    stirring ashes of our lives
    raising up the lame and dead
    by that power that's beyond our eyes

by that power that gives us might
gives us courage to overcome
our despair and hopelessness
new creatures of intercommunion

This is what we celebrate
during spring the awesome sound
of cracked cocoons rolling stones
and shouts of the forgiven resound

the splashing play of whales
future buzz of honey bees
sight for the blinded bigots
lasting peace among earth's enemies

Nonvisible and mysterious
power will surely raise the dead
will inspire our breath again
'tis the power of Easter I said

She said I think I've got it
ev'ry time I thought I'd died
the greatest secret of all
revealed to me life in death does hide

Yes life is so very good I said

Communion Within Creation

In and through this [universe] community we enter into communion with that numinous mystery. ~**Thomas Berry,** "Cosmology of Religions"

Awesome moments of communion with what is:

Suckling at my mother's breast as a babe . . .
  communion with my mother
Walking the trail in the moonlight . . .
  communion with mother nature
Kissing the one I would marry. . .
  communion with my mate
Looking down on my hometown from a plane . . .
  communion with environs
Licked by Lulu, our dog, as I studied theology . . .
  communion with a another species
Granddaughter's mercy during great pain . . .
  communion with next generations
Seeing my Blue Ridge after an absence . . .
  communion with my home
Staring into the eyes of a seagull at Caswell . . .
  communion with a strange creature
Watching Nolan bend over to kiss a flower . . .
  communion with one in communion
Hearing monks growl chants in Thai temple . . .
  communion with another tradition

Climbing in a 5000-year-old pyramid on the Nile . . .
　　communion with my ancestors
Conversing in an India village at midnight . . .
　　communion with one of 6.4 billion locals
Hearing Mama say "I love you" as she died . . .
　　communion with utter mystery
Meditating on my breathing . . .
　　communion with breath within my breath

When communion happens
　　sometimes I experience the other as a *thou*
　　sometimes I experience the *eternal thou*
And when that happens I experience
　　much more than neurological sensations
　　as I am united with the other
　　embraced in the unity of being
Sometimes I believe again
　　because trust is reborn during communion
　　as I am held in being
　　within all my communities

Is time space matter and energy are all there is?
　　These four are hardly the grand total of it all
　　Permeating them is numinous mystery
　　without which they are but so much stuff
　　with which they are consecrated being

Great communion keeps us bowing to creation
keeps us saying I give thanks for your being
With hands pressed together at the heart

people bow to greet each other with *namaste*
meaning *spirit's* at the heart of creation
    at the heart of you
    experienced in communion

Communion happens in little and big ways:

Sing a simple love song and discover yourself
    singing to all that is
Gaze at a flickering candle
    and commune with light in darkness
Watch an ant colony
    and commune with a community in action
Read the *Psalms*
    and commune with David's Lord
Hold your new baby
    and commune in unspeakable joy
See bulldozers pushing bodies into mass graves
    and commune with genocidal dying
Hear the African Children's Choir
    and commune with millions dying of AIDS
Break bread and spill wine
    and commune with the goodness of life itself

Every piece of creation is blessed is sacred
For *spirit* is revealed through each
    to be communed with
Since every created thing has a heart

Communion is the "union with" all that is
SiddhArtha and Francis knew each *other*
    is sister brother father mother
We experience union
    in communion
        with each and every one
        in creation

For in reality we are One
    and through *spirit's* power of *communion*
    we experience this fact of all facts

As Thomas says in the beginning

"In and through this universe community
    we enter into communion
    with that numinous mystery"

. . . at the heart of everything that is.

Oh I Don't Know

Two lonely leaves hanging from a limb
tossed in the early winter wind
considering the day of their fall
What will happen after we descend

Said one to the other: What if
when we land there is nothing more
nothing except we rot away
Wouldn't that be an awful shame

Said the other: Oh I don't know
From dust to dust is the promise
and I'm sort of fascinated
by the process of changing form

The first: Isn't *transformation*
a word for raving romantics
who believe in happy endings
We're about to experience death

Said the second: Oh I don't know
The way the word *death* comes to me
is something like what happened when
dinosaurs died in the 60s

and vegetation really thrived
That is the big picture on death
I guess it all makes sense to me

thinking of what comes after us

The first: Maybe the universe
and the earth will figure it out
All we have to do is be blown
And soon they did float to the ground

The second: That was sort of neat
an experience we've not had
First: Yea here we are yet alive
Is death only a metaphor

Oh I don't know said the second
I'm sort of enjoying the view
From down here it does give us a
new perspective on everything

Then asked the first: Do humans think
about what happens after death
Oh I don't know said the second
But they don't need to be afraid

Two lonely leaves hanging from a limb
tossed in the early winter wind
considering the day of their fall
What will happen after we descend

~printed in *Poetry GSO* (Poetry Greensboro)

Aussie Wisdom

What must I know before I go?
What will I do if I have to?
What will I be if really me?

These are the questions they tell us
we must answer if we live in
the world of civilization.

But you know, mate,
they don't know their
head from their bum.

I think it is more a question
of seeing life's answer in the
mystery of communion.

Rich Is Not . . . Rich Is

rich is not
how much you have
or who you are.

rich is
communing with
the heart of creation.

Yaaaa from a Universe Shrink

The therapy of self-acceptance
is on the rise in self-centered cultures
leading to delusion the poor souls
that want to believe I can
if I will just accept myself

But you are not created that way
What you can do is accept the other
outside the boundary of your skin
be they human or non-human
be she the universe herself

The fact is you are accepted
by her who is not yourself
You just show up in the flow
of this universe on the move
from creation to creation

That's really quite enough
don't you think when you think
You are at just this moment
sublimely nestled in the flow
of the cosmic oneness

But I don't feel accepted
Who said you were supposed to
Since you are now in the flow
be that the meaning of your life

121

a part of the ongoing goingonness

One more time let me say
she accepts just who you are
Just try to get off the earth
Try to get out of the universe
Your acceptance is complete

So please get it straight
Look up from your navel
and live the way the rest
of creation is living
like trees cows and neutrinos

Get on with your life
Look up and out and live
because you are accepted
by all that was and is and will be
even though you don't feel like it

If you still yearn for acceptance
let me say it one last time
You Are Always Already Accepted
YAAAA That's all you need to know
Your self-acceptance obsession be gone

That will be $400 please

Amazing Grace*

Amazing grace, ten thousand times,
has touched the heart of me;
I once was lost but now am found,
was blind but now I see.

Through mighty, awesome turns in life
I have already come;
'tis grace that makes me whole through faith,
and grace will lead me on.

Amazingly, since primal star,
grace joined this voice of mine
with all creation near and far
to celebrate sublime.

When we've been journeyed all our days
by grace till breath is gone,
we'll no less yearn to sing its praise
than when we'd first begun.

* adapted from **John Newton**, 1779

Love All of Nature

The universe is a swirl of nature,
as the stars and sea and jungle adhere.

There are other parts of this cosmic world:
we humans were into nature hurled.

A tad less than angels we humans are,
homo sapiens as good as a star.

Ev'ry bit a part of the universe,
and not one thing is in any way worse.

20k orangutan kin remain,
begging us not to take their kind in vain.

During extinctions there must surely come
from the heart of us humans more freedom

To care for all *a tad less than angels*,
delighting in them, reversing farewells.

Is it not our natural role to care
if keener awareness we humbly bear?

Mothers love most the child in greatest need
'cause security is not guaranteed.

Center of all until Copernicus,
humans' show no longer, except to bless.

Toynbee's line and Dietrich's prison quote,
"world thus come of age," is very remote.

We humans have not come of age for sure
and won't until we love all of nature.

Intercommunion

Intercommunion is Born of Communion with Creation

Intercommunion . . .
    is the way life is, what essentially is
    is the fundamental fact of our oneness as creation
    is interconnectedness and interdependence
    is born of an experience of communion
    is a universe-community-individual affair

Intercommunion is Conscious Participation with Creation

Intercommunion . . .
    is a covenantal *yes* to creation
    is an I-thou, not an I-it, relationship with what is
    is a demonstration of unity, soul to soul
    is lived out in authentic community
    is an expression of deep care for creation
    is manifest in local/planetary sacrificial service
    is the lifestyle of reconciliation

In sum:

    At one with the heart of creation
        – with the power of *being* –
        we experience *communion* . . .
    that motivates us toward *intercommunion*.

Just *Yes* or *No*

I share the genes of a banana I found out
on NOVA tonight and felt connected
in a new way to all of life.

Found out we humans are 99 point 9 percent
the same gene-wise and I felt connected
in new ways to the 6 billion.

I did not find out tonight how we humans
really do differ from the animals
or from the other forms of life.

I think it has something to do with the way we
perceive truth, how we respond, how we choose,
and what are our basic values.

It is much more than species, nation, religion,
education, relative wealth, power –
we humans decide *no* or *yes*.

Are we better than all the non-humans,
more evolved than rocks, worms, and waterfalls,
more conscious than bacteria?

With the 6 billion there's hardly a difference,
only color and a few other things,
not enough to shake a stick at.

The *yes* and *no* don't seem to be any big deal
till we consider the human venture
and impact on the earth venture.

What Gets Me Down

What gets me down these days is
our pattern of consumption
our use of the earth
our abuse of the ozone
our denial of destroying the ecosystems

plus . . .
    war
    poverty
    wealth
    HIV/AIDS
    addiction
    population
    hate

But as Søren says
authentic despair
has within it the cure –
possibility and necessity –
the power of conversion
which is grounded in *spirit*

To think we are going
to deal with all this
without radical conversion of
    spirit
    values
    priorities
    actions
is the biggest illusion

Let despair intensify
until we grieve for all
until we believe
and act like
we really are one planet
immersed in sacrificial possibility

Is There Any Hope at All?

Is there any hope at all
in our present situation
or are we but doomed
to planetary destruction?

There's nothing much to offer
    except
mysterious fullness
endless possibility
    and
creative vitality.

Oh, my God,
nothing more?

Our Home Sweet Home

Earth is not just a planet
not just a place in space
x distance from here and there

Our home is the earth
the place where our heart is
there's no place like home

Earth is trillions of home-ones
who live and have their being
on and in her wondrous realm

Lord knows we love our home
sustained and united in her kingdom
of communion one with another

But we feel threatened of late
by our disregard for the way
we have treated our Mother

Thus many are losing their home
many are being denied her riches
many are being denied their birthright

As all her children we dare to see
what's happening to our kin
and are beginning to grieve and act

For we know deep down
that if more and more lose their home
earth for all of us is threatened

But we *can* go home again
if we love Mother Earth
and find our fulfillment in her's

So let's sing with Irving . . .

God bless our planet Earth
Home that we love
Be within her and guide her
Through the night with the light from above

From the ozone to the humans
To the oceans white with foam
God bless our planet Earth
Our home sweet home

God bless our planet Earth
Our home sweet home

My Neighbor Is

My biggest neighbor is Grandfather Universe
My smallest neighbor is Little Neutrino
My oldest and farthest neighbor is Old Fireball
My neighbor I can't do without is Father Sun
My most caring neighbor is Mother Earth
My most delightful neighbors, Grand Children
My meanest neighbors are War and Poverty
My most fragile neighbor is Uncle Water
My most abused neighbor is Teen Prostitute
My most needy neighbor is HIV/AIDS Millions
My neighbor most on my mind, Dispirited Masses

"Whatever I do not do for the least of these" . . .

"If we say we love God and hate the neighbor,
          we are liars" . . .

"The second is like unto the first . . . and thy
          neighbor as thyself " . . .

"One fell among thieves and was dying in a ditch
          Two holy ones saw him and passed by
          His enemy stopped and cared for him
          Which one was the neighbor" . . .

"The earth is the Lord's and everything in it" . . .

Who can think of anything
    that's not the neighbor
Today I will make an offering
    to Brother Rain Forest
Tomorrow I will march in the streets
    for Sister Peace
The next day I'll meet
    New Folks next door

I Am

"I doubt, therefore, I am,"
Said René Descartes,
Letting loose western humanism.

But what about
"I dialogue, therefore, I am";
"I care, therefore, I am"?

Or what about
"I commune, therefore, I am";
"I intercommune, therefore, I am"?

In any case, I am I,
In relationship with all that is,
I have no doubt.

Humanism Is Bust

Merriam and Webster define a "humanist" as
one concerned about . . .
the humanities
literary culture
individual dignity and worth
self-realization through reason
a critical spirit
secular concerns characterized by the Renaissance
philosophy viewed non-theistically
and humanitarian efforts.
This is all well and good, and a bit highfalutin.

But what about their meaning of "humanism"
that says . . .
a doctrine, attitude, or way of life centered on
human interests or values?
Haven't we done this definition to death?
Hasn't human-centeredness turned in on us?
Haven't our obsessive human interests and
    values terribly tinkered with the planet?

One more meaning they list under "humanism":
a philosophy that usually rejects supernaturalism.
What does humanism put
    in supernaturalism's place?
Not much.

How do humanists talk about the

height and depth of human experience?
Their jargon seems flat, without much sap.
Whose philosophy is deeply satisfying
    the souls of us humans these days?

"Humanism" is bust,
one of the worst of the "-isms,"
one of earth's major contradictions.

What about the words
"humanist" and "humanistic"?
Like father like sons.

Coin new words
for creation's sake!
Webster and Merriam,
re-ink your quills
for goodness sake.

Beatitudes

Many say . . .
Blessed are the rich
Blessed are the powerful
Blessed are the winners
Blessed are the armed
Blessed are the comfortable
Blessed are the consumers
Blessed are the entertained
Blessed are the educated
    the developed
    the civilized
    the cultured
For they inherit their self-made kingdom

But Jesus said . . .
Blessed are the poor
Blessed are the meek
Blessed are the merciful
Blessed are the pure in heart
Blessed are the peacemakers
Blessed are they that mourn
Blessed are those like little children
Blessed are those who do my father's will
Blessed are they that lay down their lives for others
For their kingdom is heaven on earth

And I Say . . .
Blessed are all the children

all beings
human or not
Blessed are they
    not because of what they own
    not because of what they achieve
    but because they just are
    – each of value as is –
Blessed are they
For they *are already* the good creation

Whichever

I bow to *spirit* at the heart of creation –
always already present in creation –
whether I bow to you personally,
or to my kin on this piedmont,
or to all Earth's creatures,
or Sun's zillion neutrinos.

Humans have circled up around campfires
since Mars came this close to planet Earth,
sharing stories of their experience
with the micro- and macrocosm,
inventing religion
out of spirituality:

Life happens to us and we experience it,
sometimes making us conscious of our *yes* or *no*,
sometimes making us at one with *spirit*.
Down deep we all know, or can know,
that the way life is, at heart,
it is transparent to *spirit*.

Whether we have been asleep or on watch,
we beings of creation have been journeyed
univers'ly by that which journeys all –
experiencing *communion*,
being at one with all,
deciding to *intercommune* –

For this purpose: that we all care for creation,
not just for self or mine, but for everything;
bowing to each as *thou* and not as *it*.
Truly, holy traditions teach
that creation is good,
meaning "heaven is in our midst."

How to draw the line of "Who is my neighbor?"
if all is very good and is connected,
if reverence and compassion for all
means responsibility for all –
bowing to and serving
all created heirs of *spirit*?

"The cosmos is *spirit's* and the fullness thereof";
we who "love *spirit* and hate the neighbor"
forget everything is *in* creation
and forget it's all "very good,"
forget that "the second
command is like unto the first."

I will bow to *spirit* and will see creation,
or bow to creation and see through to *spirit* . . .
    whichever . . .
for *spirit's* always at the heart.

VII

from *Journer*
(a journey novel)

To Begin and End the Day
(*Peter's Prayer*)

I bow to *spirit*
at the heart of creation
and to all that is

all universes
our universe
Mother Earth

and to all beings
all species
all tribes
my friends and enemies
my colleagues
my family
and to my own being

I bow to all as *thou*
the human *thou*

the non-human *thou*
the *eternal thou*
I bow to all this day
Namaste

Contemporary "Prologue"

Peter saw that the Judeo-Christian scriptures were talking about the power of the *spirit* of God and *spirit* of Christ as the presence of the *holy spirit* in any time, from the very beginning to the futuric "omega point." Out of this context he understood and paraphrased the "Prologue" to the *Gospel of John* (1:1-19):

> In the beginning was *spirit*, the source of authentic being. *Spirit* shines from the heart of creation. Nothing has ever been able to hide its glory.

> A man was called by *spirit* to witness to its power, so that all might understand the profundity of being in creation. He testified to this central fact: *spirit* is in creation but seldom seen, and if seen, seldom becomes one's point of reference.

> However, some have seen and bowed to its transforming power and have been reborn, as it were, conceived by *spirit* – thus its children – even virgin born.

Spirit is always already present among us, the central dynamism of creation, offering *its* grace and truth to all beings as sheer gift that never stops giving.

We all can come to know its presence and power through ones who lived at one with and became transparent to *spirit* – if you saw them, you saw *spirit*, eternally present.

And we too, bowing to *spirit*, saying "yes" to *spirit* as it encounters us, we too become transparent ones, transparent to its presence.

That Which Will Not Deconstruct

You call it what you will . . .
spirit is awe-fully real
it graciously fulfills
gives wonder and passion
it is true and certain
earning our faith and trust
it is the greatest loss
run to *it* or from *it*
all reveals *its* presence
all's transparent to *it*
all is therefore holy
spirit permeates all
consecrates creation
spirit's primordial
it is never absent
spirit is here for e'er

VIII

from *Daily Spirit Journal* (vol. I)

December 22   **All Are Virgin Born**

> In the beginning Jesus was born,
> like us,
> that we might be like him,
> purely human.
>
> All are virgin born,
> says the gospeler in John: 1. . . .

December 23   **All Are Born Again**

How silently, how silently, the wondrous gift is given;
so God imparts to human hearts the blessings of his heaven.

. . . where meek souls will receive him,
still the dear Christ enters in. ~**Phillips Brooks**

> Dear Christ enters in –
> love is born again . . .
> the gift of heaven.

We receive it still –
silently . . . our souls
and hearts are filled.

All are born again –
silently God's gift
of love enters in.

December 24   **The Christmas *Word***

The *word* is at the heart of creation.
The *word* is historical.
The *word* is in the hearts of all those
who have said *yes* to its power
throughout all ages
– even before Jesus –
and in all places –
even where Christianity
has never been.

May 9   **Solitary Bird**

. . . it aims its beak to the skies
. . . it flies to the highest point
. . . it doesn't suffer for company
. . . it does not have a definite color
. . . it sings very softly

~adapted from **St. John of the Cross**

146

May 31   **Getting Unstuck**

The *spirit* of the universe
is revealing we are stuck
– evolutionarily speaking –
in our human-centeredness,
devolving earth community
and holding it back.

Spirit is about
getting us unstuck.

June 5   **We Are Experiencing *Spirit***

We are experiencing *spirit*

When something radical, total, and unconditional
    is demanded of us,

When we hear we can go on, in spite of all,
    we are experiencing *spirit*.

When relased to be slave to no thing and free for all,
    we are experiencing *spirit*.

When we see and respond to creation's suffering,
    we are experiencing *spirit*.

June 10   **Means of Grace**

Marriage is about *communion* (deep life in *spirit*):
to keep your *covenant* and mission of *care* alive,
remember "home" is . . .

> a communion place
> a caring place
> a forgiving place
> a deep breathing place
> a dialogue place
> a fun place
> a healing place
> a sacramental place

. . . marriage and home are means of grace.

~from remarks at Spain wedding of J&V

June 19   ***Spirit* re Relationship**

Spirit reveals itself

in relationship
through grace

in disrelationship
through judgment

both of which
are finally gracious

148

June 27　　**Resurrectional Time**

> All time begins
> in a moment
> then comes the end
> The moment dead
> after dying
> starts up again

June 28　　**From an Art Perspective**

Look at that tree.
It's different from all the other trees.
Every tree's a piece of art.

Look at that cat . . . and that child. . . .
Look at that HIV/AIDS person.
She's different from all the other . . . .

But none of these pieces of art
will bring anything close to the price
of a piece of art at a Sotheby's Auction.

IX

from *Daily Spirit Journal* (vol. II)

November 3   **thou Is Thou**

I have heard it said,
"Be at one with nature to be at one with humanity."
And "Be at one with self to be at one with others."

> I'd rather say,
> "All is one.
> Union with any
> is union with all.
> In a transparent sense,
> thou is Thou."

Somewhere it is said:
"If you have been united with one
        of the least of these,
you have been united with the eternal thou."

December 11   **How Do We Begin To Love . . .**

How do we begin to love in such a way that births peace?

Tell someone in your family you love them,
    someone who would be shocked to hear it.
Call or write someone you dislike or despise
    and ask for their forgiveness,
      even if you think he or she is to blame.
Practice tonglen meditation regularly,
    breathing in the pain of particular persons,
    organizations, cities, nations, species, planet,
    and then breathing out to them peace and love.
Adopt a "leper," someone who has pieces of his
    or her spirit rotting away.

Christmas is the reality of love which births peace.

~from 1994 Christmas letter

December 18   **The Gift Love Brings**

    Mysterious power gives life,
    takes it away, and
    loves us in between.

    Especially at Christmas *it* heals
    our broken lives with
    what we're longing for.

Acceptance is the gift *love* brings
creating a new heart
through *its* grace event:

In a moment the great *aha* . . .
I'm transformed, newborn,
snow-pure. *Love divine.*

~from 1993 Christmas letter

December 25   **We Pray in Jesus' Name**

We celebrate the birth of Jesus
with that first community of faith,
made up of diverse worshippers –
wise men, shepherds, and animals –
who journeyed toward a star.

We celebrate the Jesus *word*
with the followers of Jesus in history,
who have embodied new life,
demonstrated new community,
and have championed grace and peace.

We give thanks the *word's* in history
and has come to and belongs to all,
because the *word* rises out of the way life is:
meaning, all is good, the past is approved,
each is accepted, and the future is open.

152

We celebrate the *word's*
pronouncement that all creation
is new and going somewhere,
not old and going out of being.
The *word* fills us with hope.

So, on this holy day,
in this holy place,
with these holy ones,
we give heartfelt thanks
. . . especially in Jesus' name. *Amen*

~from 2005 Christmas letter

March 5   **So Journey On . . .**

Religions mark human journey events
that have just evented us again:
Wednesday we welcomed Clara into our world;
Thursday we sent cousin Susan out.

Mystified by how we come, be, and go . . .
we journey on.
In eternity before birth,
during life,
and after death . . .
we journey on.

How can anything in being ever go out?
Spirit has more room –

the universes *it* traverses . . .
so journey on . . .
without end. *Amen.*

April 16   **"Enough! the Resurrection"**

> . . . Enough! the Resurrection:
> In a flash, at a trumpet crash,
> I am all at once what Christ is,
> since he was what I am, and
> Me, Jack, joke, piece of clay,
> patch, sliver, broken piece of s____,
> Am really a diamond . . .
> by "God."

~adapted from **Gerald Manley Hopkins's**
"That Nature Is a Heraclitean Fire"

April 24   **Whose Am I?**

> Whose am I if none of these:
> Neither Christian, Jew, nor Moslem.
> Not of East, West, North, or South;
> Not of Nature nor the stars of Heaven.
>
> Not of Europe nor the U.S. of A.;
> Not of this world nor the next.
> Neither body nor soul, I belong to *spirit*:
> The One I seek, call, see, and know.

~adapted from **Rumi's**, "Divan of Shems of Tabriz, 31"

May 10   **Quantum Spirituality**

A quantum haiku for all seasons:

> *imagine being*
> *in the actuality*
> *of utter oneness*

June 12   **Bow Down, Look Around**

You're left with yourself all the time. . . . But you've got to get down to your own god and "your own temple. . . ." [I]t's all down to you. . . . ~**John Lennon**

> You got to bow down
> to your own god in your holy place
> to find the meaning of life.
> If that one won't sustain you,
> keep going, deeper. . . deeper.
> Or start looking around you
> till you see signs of the One
> in all this hallowed space.
> You got to bow down, look around.

Bow down in either paradigm of spirituality. **Namaste**.

Index of Titles

Books by the Author

By Cosmic Design
Spirit Poems (1974-2006)

Daily Spirit Journal (volume II)
Quotes and Reflections for 365 Days (2006)

Daily Spirit Journal (volume I)
Quotes and Reflections for 365 Days (2005)

Journer
A contemporary spirit journey like unto
Herman Hesse's novelette *Siddhartha* (2005)

At One With the Heart of Creation
Reflections and Verse on the Spirit Journey (2004)
with Lynda Cock; foreword by Thomas Berry

Our Universal Spirit Journey
Reflection and Verse for Creation's Sake (2002)
foreword by Thomas Berry

Motivation for the Great Work
Forty Meaty Meditations for the Secular-Religious
foreword by Thomas Berry (2000)

The Transparent Event
Post-modern Christ Images (2nd ed., 2001)
comment by Bishop James K. Mathews

Called To Be
A Spirit Odyssey (2nd ed., 2000)
comments by Wanda Urbanska
and James Dodson

Co-edited

Bending History
Selected Talks of Joseph W. Mathews (2005)
John L. Epps, general editor

Brother Joe
A 20th Century Apostle (2006)
by Bishop James K. Mathews

About the Author

John P. Cock is an author/editor, a speaker, spirit journey retreat guide, and daily reflection blogger. In addition to the USA, he has lived and worked in Australia, Indonesia, Malaysia, and India.

E-mail
tranScribebooks@triad.rr.com

or visit web page and blog
www.tranScribebooks.com
www.reJourney.blogspot.com

Cover Designer

Tara McDermott is a graphic designer from Dubuque, Iowa, where she renders art, designs covers and interior art, and provides photo research.

www.ingramcontent.com/pod-product-compliance
Lightning Source LLC
Chambersburg PA
CBHW031318040426
42443CB00005B/128